I0116158

ISBN 978-0-9803348-1-4

Front cover Pieter Brueghel: The Triumph of
Death 1562

EVERY DAY IS 9/11

New Proposals for Iraq

© Barrie Machin

SHIMMERING PIONEER BOOKS

Every day is 9/11

Copyright © 2007 Barrie Machin

ISBN 978-0-9803348-1-4

All rights reserved.

No part of this book may be reproduced or transmitted in any form or by any means without written permission of the author.

TABLE OF CONTENTS

INTRODUCTION

This book is about the U.S. coalition occupation of Iraq and the failure to rebuild the infrastructure of the country as promised.

The war was started on the basis of a lie and is a continuation of a history of error. The American Middle East policy is a kind of Basil Fawlty escalation of compounding errors.[1]

U.S. foreign policy is not consistently idealistic and, in many examples of foreign policy since WWII, it has often subverted the ideals of democracy. The principles of American democracy, despite statements to the contrary, were abandoned in both Iraq wars. The U.S. supported Hussein[2] in the past and currently supports tyrannical regimes.[3]

---

[1] Famous BBC series, 1975-1979, in which an arrogant, inept and paranoid hotel owner lies to cover up the failures of his hotel. As one lie is discovered he covers it with another, until an absurd, out of control, situation develops. Like Bush his historical perspective is as faulty as his name..

[2] http://www.hoover.org/publications/digest/3063121.html

This article argues that the U.S. policy is defensible because it supports the lesser evil and justifies the earlier support of Hussein on these grounds, but it glosses over the fact that U.S. interference too often creates the greater evil it later opposes. In my view the defeat of the Soviet Union might have been achieved

How much better it would have been to remove Hussein at the beginning of the Iran-Iraq war instead of cynically supporting him and his tyrannical regime, aiding and abetting his genocidal acts and stimulating fundamentalism in Iran.

This book does not imply an objection to the trial and hanging of Hussein, in my view he got better than he deserved and much better than he gave to millions of people. As an admirer of many of the fundamental principles of Buddhism, Christianity and Islam, [4] I

---

earlier had U.S. foreign policy been more consistent with its own internal values and less arbitrary.

[3] America supports dictatorships in Azerbaijan, Uzbekistan, and Kazakhstan and Pakistan. Husain Haqqani 'Bush's Hypocritical Oath, Speak No Evil' *New Republic* 02.07.05

http://www.tnr.com/doc.mhtml? i=20050207&s=haqqani020705

> *Indeed, the gap between Bush's pro-democracy rhetoric and his pro-status quo policies was illustrated during a White House meeting the president had with Musharraf in December, during which he called for "a world effort to help the Palestinians develop a state that is truly free: One that's got an independent judiciary; one that's got a civil society; one that's got the capacity to fight off the terrorists; one that allows for dissent; one in which people can vote." Ironically, most of those criteria are not met in Pakistan."*

[4] This is a complicated issue. It is possible to use great religions and their texts in many ways. In 'A deadly certitude' Steven Weinberg's review of Richard Dawkins *The god delusion* Bantam. *Times Online* January 17 2007 he says:

believe that following the Koran and admiring Saddam Hussein are mutually contradictory. Hussein used religion when it suited him not because he believed. His actions were in direct contradiction to the fundamental tenets of the Koran.

Whatever one thinks of the Muslims who blow themselves up in crowded cities in Europe or Israel or fly planes into buildings in the US, who could dispute that the certainty of their faith had something to do with it? George W. Bush and many others would have us believe that terrorism is a distortion of Islam, and that Islam is a religion of peace. Of course, it is good policy to say this, but statements about what "Islam is" make little sense. Islam, like all other religions, was created by people, and there are potentially as many different versions of Islam as there are people who profess to be Muslims. ... I don't know on what ground one can say that a peaceable well-intentioned person like Abdus Salam was any more a true Muslim than the murderous holy warriors of Hezbollah and Islamic Jihad, the clerics throughout the world of Islam who incite hatred and violence, and those Muslims who demonstrate against supposed insults to their faith,...

It would seem that people will find any excuse to fight see Jonathan Swift 1726 *Gulliver's Travels* Part 4 – 'A Voyage to the Country of the Houyhnhnms'.

I think we have to find common ground and assume that the majority of Muslims and Christians want peace not war. It would be better if there were less religious interference in politics. I believe in the secular state. I do think we have a distorted view of Iraq if Britain had been reported this way in WWII the ordinary life and opinion of people would not have appeared at all.

I assume that most Iraqis favour peace, reject extremism and want to get on with their lives as we all do.

I propose that the U.S. and other members of the coalition withdraw their troops now and instead concentrate on a vastly increased aid program not the paltry sum currently proposed by Bush. Initially this would replace the stolen 23 billion. The cost of the war so far is between $250 and $350 billion. This is monstrous. A fraction of this could have been used to pay Saddam to leave and have money left over to totally transform the region. I suppose it is always easier to raise money for bullets than bread.

At the same time the Iraqi government should be encouraged to commence a program of consultation, with Iraqi anthropologists, sociologists, historians and all leaders of opposing groups and factions. The government can also, via mobile phone services, consult all Iraqis.

There should be a regional summit with the leaders of all regional powers.

In other words I propose a radical change of U.S. foreign policy direction, back to the original intention of the Monroe Doctrine- no direct intervention in the affairs of other nations and the cessation of support for totalitarian regimes.

Most importantly, since the arms race is fuelling conflicts in the region and elsewhere, the coalition should pursue a universal reduction in arms sales and continued nuclear disarmament as proposed in the Treaty on the Non-proliferation of Nuclear Weapons (NPT) 1970.

To argue against the war and its fundamental perpetrators is not an attempt to demonize Americans. I argue against all demonization, including nations belonging to the so-called 'the axis of evil'. There are good and bad regimes and demonstrably evil regimes like Fascism and Stalinism. [5] But generic stereotyping serves little purpose especially when applied to a complex of different regimes and cultures.

Opposition to U.S. war actions does not imply approval of other murderous actions or terrorism. Nor does it forget the contribution America made in the Second World War or its opposition to Soviet Communism.

To be opposed to the U.S. occupation is not to despise America or Americans nor does such opposition presuppose an admiration of Hamas or Bin Laden or any other group. The Hamas[6] failure to recognize Israel is both morally wrong and totally and suicidally unrealistic. Even if we can understand the context within which it operates the logical conclusion of Hamas policy is MAD (mutually assured destruction). Vendetta is out of place in the modern

---

[5] There are definite criteria for such regimes e.g. mass exterminations, organized violence etc., see Alan Bullock 1991 *Hitler And Stalin: Parallel Lives* Harper Collins. Holocaust denial, on its own, does not qualify.

[6] Hamas and Hezbollah:
http://www.beliefnet.com/story/195/story_19586_1.html . The central problem posed by both groups is their threat to destroy Israel.

world; new-fashioned weapons scale it up to unimaginable horror. The choice is coexistence or non-existence.

Legislation for crimes against humanity genocide and war crimes in the International Criminal Court should be strengthened and evenly applied to all nations, whether committed by the coalition of the willing, [7] Israel, Palestinians, Hezbollah, Hamas, or other factions in Iraq and Lebanon. Some U.S. leaders have committed, or are implicated in, culpable criminal acts. [8] I condemn all illegal acts committed in the name of other peoples and nations. All war crimes are equal. The values we supposedly uphold cannot be defended and maintained by their subversion in the field of war. We, and our values, are diminished when this happens. Our common humanity and survival depends on the continued

---

[7] I do not link the U.S. irrevocably with Israel.

[8] Hersh, Seymour M. (foreword) 2005 in Scott Ritter: *Iraq Confidential: The Untold Story of the Intelligence Conspiracy to Undermine the UN and Overthrow Saddam Hussein*, Nation Books, -2004. *Chain of Command: The Road from 9/11 to Abu Ghraib.* HarperCollins. -1998. *Against All Enemies: Gulf War Syndrome: The War Between America's Ailing Veterans and Their Government.* Ballantine Books. -1997 *The Dark Side of Camelot.* Little, Brown & Company. -1991 The *Samson Option: Israel's Nuclear Arsenal and American Foreign Policy.* Random House. -1986 *The Target Is Destroyed: What Really Happened to Flight 007 and What America Knew About It.* Random House. -1983 *The Price of Power: Kissinger in the Nixon White House.* Simon & Schuster. Excerpts from *The Price of Power* hosted by Third World Traveler

evolution and application of universal standards of law, justice, equality and mercy.

To those, who might say that one must be realistic, that all nations act in their self interest, that if we did not supply weapons then someone else will, that dictatorships occur with or without our support etc. etc., I say that the problem with this Realpolitik is that its trajectory is tragedy for all. It is a Realpolitik, which guarantees that our self-interest is ultimately not served. In a narrow historical perspective it may have limited application. But this old Realpolitik will destroy us all.

It is possible to change direction and substitute a more principled approach including the support of arms control, and strengthening the United Nations. I propose a new Reasonpolitik [9] and rejection of policies, which are leading us, inexorably, to an abyss.

---

[9] There is an urgent necessity for us all to join hands and face the threatening cataclysm which global warming poses. We would do this if threatened by aliens form outer space. This is no different. The aliens, in this case, are our inner demons. I am reminded of a Brueghel print showing human beings committing the usual deadly sins ignoring the tidal wave which is about to break over them. Bush can be compared to King Canute. See Kate Ravilious 2007 '2100: A world of wild weather' 18 January *NewScientist.com* news service, and *The Times* January 18, 2007 '*It's five minutes to Armageddon, and Hawking tells the world to wake up*' Mark Henderson, Science Editor *Climate change is as great a threat to the world as international terrorism and nuclear war, Professor Stephen Hawking said yesterday.*

CHAPTER ONE THE STOLEN BILLIONS

The Documentary - Iraq's Missing Billions

'THE FREE FRAUD ZONE'

In a hospital room in Diwaniyah, a new-born baby is struggling to breathe. She urgently needs oxygen but the hospital has no suitable equipment. Instead, staff have made a crude arrangement of suction pipes and are holding a tube to her nose. "This treatment is worse than primitive. It's not even medicine", despairs a doctor as the little girl dies. This hospital was meant to have benefited from a $4 million refit. But the standard of work is terrible. Raw sewage leaks into the kitchens and operating theatres. New light fittings have melted. Ants crawl around on the floor. Little wonder people here feel betrayed. "This terrible hospital will make my child worse", complains one parent. " As trustees, we did a very poor job," admits Frank Willis, a senior member of the CPA and one of Bremer's top officials. "We should have spent the money on the Iraqi people, rather than putting it in the pockets of foreign business." Contracts were negotiated fast and furiously. There was no oversight of projects and security was appalling. "We played football with bricks of hundred dollar bills." As word spread of the kind of money that could be made in Iraq, foreign contractors flocked. "These were people who had no interest in fostering democracy. They had no interest even in carrying out their instructions. What they were interested in was simply making a profit", states lawyer Alan Grayson.

Companies like Custer Battles billed for work they hadn't done and charged the CPA a 1000% mark up for their expenses. They spray painted abandoned Iraqi vehicles and hired them to the government at an exorbitant rate. But despite undeniable evidence of fraud, the government took no steps to recover the money. Custer was even allowed to keep their contracts. "The government wants to foster the view that things are going well in Iraq. Coming down hard on war profiteering is inconsistent with that goal", explains Grayson. While dodgy contractors were making mil lions, the Iraqi people were left paying the price. According to the United States' own figures, Iraq's essential services are worse than before the war. It's producing less electricity, oil or clean water. "Nobody cares or listens to us", complains one man. The coalition was due to hand over whatever money was left to the incoming government. But instead of trying to leave them as much as possible, the CPA went on an extraordinary spending spree. "There was a push to spend the money that was remaining", states fraud investigator Ginger. One official was given seven million dollars and told to spend it in seven days. Contractors complained that they were being pressured to spend the money fast. In the end, only three and a half billion was handed over to the new government. Iraq's own money is spent and America says once the additional money pledged is gone, there will be no more. In the words of Frank Willis: "Our opportunity is gone. We blew it." (Guardian Films 23 March 2006] from http://www.journeyman.tv/?lid=56149 you can see some of the documentary on this site, also:

9

http://www.cbc.ca/passionateeyesunday/feature 011006.htm l.

In Sept. 2003, on television, President Bush promised to restore basic services, such as electricity and water, and to build new schools, roads, and medical clinics, see report in the Independent http://wwwnews.independent.co.uk/world/middle east/article350776.ece.

Of 23 billion dollars, mostly Iraqi money, stored in Federal Reserve Banks in New York, twelve billion in notes were flown from St Andrew's Airport, for Iraqi reconstruction. It has been stolen. The main benefactors, apparently, were GOP supporters.[10]

When I watched this documentary I was moved to anger and outrage. I understood the anger of the insurgents. Momentarily I felt that I too could take up arms against such sanctimonious blackguards. I could imagine taking extreme measures against such outrageous, disgusting and murderous hypocrites. Imagine if I could feel this, I, who have espoused peace all my life, what would the victims of these crimes and injustices feel?

However let me be clear from the outset, despite this emotional response, I do not condone violence or terrorist acts.

---

[10] 'Why the US Is Not Leaving Iraq: The Booming Business of War Profiteers' Prof. Ismael Hossein-zadeh *Global Research, January 12, 2007*

10

As a result of this vile theft Iraqi children are dying in thousands.

The fraudulent contractors are murderers and should be brought to trial. Those who flew out money to such thieves should be brought to trial.

People like John Howard the Australian Prime Minister, who support the occupation and thereby the crimes committed under its aegis, suffer from a form of collective amnesia and need a history lesson.

CHAPTER TWO THE IRAQ-IRAN WAR

In the Iraq instigated war against Iran, one of the most brutal of the twentieth century, President Reagan gave his full backing to Saddam Hussein, see

http://en.wikipedia.org/wiki/Iran-Iraq_War.

WMD

Western countries and U.S.S.R. supported Saddam Hussein and provided him with the means to produce weapons of mass destruction and underground nuclear shelters.

Many schools were destroyed in air- raids and thousands of children killed,
http://en.wikipedia.org/wiki/U.S._support_for_Iraq_during_the_Iran-Iraq_war **states**:

> *Iraq's army was primarily armed with weaponry it had purchased from the Soviet Union and its satellites in the preceding decade. During the war, it purchased billions of dollars worth of advanced equipment from the Soviet Union, France, [28] as well as from the People's Republic of China, Egypt , Germany, and other sources (including Europe) and facilities for making and/or enhancing chemical weapons). Germany [29] along with other Western countries (among them United Kingdom, France, Spain (Explosivos Alaveses), Canada, Italy and*

the United States) provided Iraq with biological and chemical weapons technology and the precursors to nuclear capabilities (Wikipedia).

The U.S. sold Iraq $200 million in helicopters, which were used by the Iraqi military in the war. These were the only direct U.S.-Iraqi military sales and were valued to be about 0.6% of Iraq's conventional weapons imports during the war. [30] Ted Keppel of ABC Nightline reported the following, however, on June 9, 1992: "It is becoming increasingly clear that George Bush Sr. [11], operating largely behind the scenes throughout the 1980s, initiated and supported much of the financing, intelligence, and military help that built Saddam's Iraq into [an aggressive power]" and "Reagan/Bush administrations permitted — and frequently encouraged — the flow of money, agricultural credits, dual-use technology, chemicals, and weapons to Iraq." The Reagan Administration secretly began to allow Jordan, Saudi Arabia, Kuwait and Egypt to transfer to Iraq American howitzers, helicopters, bombs and other weapons. These shipments were done without the approval of the U.S. Congress and were in clear violation of the Arms Export Control Act as well as international law. [31] Reagan personally asked Italy's Prime Minister Guilio Andreotti to channel arms to Iraq. [32]

---

[11] Thus President Bush's father helped create Hussein's military might and capacity to produce WMD.

The United States, United Kingdom, and Germany also provided "dual use" technology (computers, engines, etc.) that allowed Iraq to expand its missile program and radar defenses. The U.S. Commerce Department, in violation of procedure, gave out licenses to companies for $1.5 billion in dual-use items to be sent to Iraq. The State Department was not informed of this. Over 1 billion of these authorized items were trucks that were never delivered. The rest consisted of advanced technology. Iraq's Soviet-made Scuds had their ranges expanded as a result. [33]

In December 2002, Iraq's 1,200 page Weapons Declaration revealed a list of Eastern and Western corporations and countries, as well as individuals, that exported a total of 17,602 tons of chemical precursors to Iraq in the past two decades. By far, the largest suppliers of precursors for chemical weapons production were in Singapore (4,515 tons), the Netherlands (4,261 tons), Egypt (2,400 tons), India (2,343 tons), and Federal Republic of Germany (1,027 tons). One Indian company, Exomet Plastics (now part of EPC Industrie) sent 2,292 tons of precursor chemicals to Iraq. The Kim Al-Khaleej firm, located in Singapore and affiliated to United Arab Emirates, supplied more than 4,500 tons of VX, Sarin, and mustard gas precursors and production equipment to Iraq. [36]

According to this article the Germans built mustard gas facilities and an American firm supplied the chemicals to produce sarin, another supplied tons of mustard gas.

CNN carries an article about the companies which
supplied Iraq,
http://www.cnn.com/2003/LAW/01/17/iraq.chemical.suit/index.html: 'Gulf
War veterans suing companies for chemical exports'
Phil Hirschkorn and Richard Roth CNN *New York
Bureau* Friday, January 17, 2003.

BIOLOGICAL AGENTS

The U.S. also exported 70 shipments of active
biological agents including anthrax and West Nile
virus. (The facility Powell pointed to at the UN to
justify the war may have been a facility the U.S. knew
well, some say that the U.S. may have helped fund
and fit it for anthrax).

Thus the U.S. actively supported Iraq's program of
WMD, including nuclear facilities.

Iran-Gate showed that five billion had been given
in secret deals to finance the war indirectly (Friedman
1993 *The Spider's Web: The Secret History of How
the White House Illegally Armed Iraq,*
http://www.namebase.org/sources/UL.html):

> *According to the Washington Post, the CIA
> began in 1984 secretly to give Iraq intelligence
> that Iraq used to "calibrate" its mustard gas
> attacks on Iranian troops. In August, the CIA
> establishes a direct Washington-Baghdad
> intelligence link, and for 18 months, starting in
> early 1985, the CIA provided Iraq with "data from
> sensitive U.S. satellite reconnaissance
> photography...to assist Iraqi bombing raids." The*

Post's source said that this data was essential to Iraq's war effort. [37]

Donald Rumsfeld was a keen supporter of Hussein and visited him and embraced him on 24th March 1984, the day after the United Nations reported the use of mustard gas on Iran:
(http://www.awitness.org/journal/Saddamrumsfeld.html).

At the same time the U.S. and Israel separately supplied much of Iran's weaponry too (see Iran-Contra affair and Bush Senior's role[12] http://en.wikipedia.org/wiki/IranContra Af).

---

[12] Supplying both sides is a tradition http://www.threeworldwars.com/world-war-2/ww2-background.htm 'What Really Caused World War 2? The Lead Up to World War 2'

It is an interesting and revealing fact of history that three other members of the Board of Governors of the American I.G. were tried and convicted as German "war criminals" for their crimes "against humanity," during World War II, while serving on the Board of Governors of I.G. Farben. None of the Americans who sat on the same board with those convicted were ever tried as "war criminals" even though they participated in the same decisions as the Germans. It appears that it is important whether your nation wins or loses the war as to whether or not you are tried as a "war criminal."

It was in 1939, during the year that Germany started the war with its invasions of Austria and Poland, that Standard Oil of New Jersey loaned I.G. Farben $20 million of high-grade aviation gasoline.

The two largest German tank manufacturers were Opel, a wholly owned subsidiary of General Motors and controlled by the J.P. Morgan firm, and the Ford subsidiary of the Ford Motor Company.

CHAPTER THREE THE LEGACY

In this 1980-88 Iraq-Iran war as many as 750,000 Iranian soldiers, and hundreds and thousands of civilian men, women, and children perished:

> *Countless waves of untrained Iranian boy-soldiers armed only with plastic keys purportedly guaranteeing entry to heaven blew themselves up[13] by the tens of thousands clearing mine fields or died charging into artillery barrages worthy of Verdun or Stalingrad.*

> *Iraqi missiles crashed through the night to spread terror among Iranian city dwellers hundreds of miles from the front (case study*

---

[13] I do not however approve of sacrificing children in this way or encouraging them to be suicide bombers. If the society believes it is necessary let the old men do it, not the young and susceptible. Such encouragement to suicide is a corruption of youthful idealism and against the tenets of Islam. These are dreadful sacrifices and many abhor them because of their religious basis and because their parents seemed to have encouraged it. It is puzzling but not uncommon and not restricted to Islam. Historically suicide and heroic sacrifice has often been used in face of superior invading forces and Christians also believe they will go to heaven for acts, which can include suicidal defence against overwhelming force.

Iran-Iraq   War   Jonathan   C.   Randall
http://www.crimesofwar.org/thebook/iran-iraq-war.html).

Amongst the casualties it is said that there were 200,000 amputees and maybe 100,000 victims of Iraq's chemical weapons. Many thousands, including children, are still dying from the effects of the war:

> *As well as the 52,000 chemical victims – both civilian and army – who are suffering severe long-term effects from the chemicals, there are another 40,000 with low-level exposure who will probably develop complications in coming years. These forgotten victims, the innocent civilians in Saddam's greatest chemical attack have been ignored by his trial (The Chemical Victims of Iran: the forgotten casualties of the Iran-Iraq war Kamin Mohammadi source: CASMII* http://www.campaigniran.org/casmii/index.php?_q=node/623 *Sunday, November 26, 2006).*

> *British geneticist Christine Gosden visited Halabjah ten years after the attack. Forensic evidence she gathered showed survivors suffering from horrifying genetic defects, skin lesions, respiratory ailments, unusually high rates of aggressive cancers and miscarriages, birth deformities such as cleft palates and harelips, lung disorders, and heart disease (Iran-Iraq   War   Jonathan   C.   Randal:* http://www.crimesofwar.org/thebook/iran-iraq-war.html).

Despite this the United States voted against a 1986 UN resolution condemning these acts.

We would have no hesitation in recognizing and condemning the responsibility of the any government or business, which supplied Hitler with weapons and poisonous gas. Neither should we now hesitate in condemning the countries, which provided Iraq with WMD. The International Court of Justice is clear, http://www.crimesofwar.org/thebook/intl-vs-internal.html:

> The International Court of Justice has held that a foreign State is responsible for the conduct of a faction in a civil war if (a) the faction is a de facto agent of the foreign State or (b) the foreign State otherwise orders it to commit certain acts.

The war cost Iran $350 billion and the country is still recovering. The present Iranian president Mahmoud Ahmadinejad is a veteran of that war. Thus far the coalition of the willing has not admitted its complicity in these matters and has kept silent about them. Given their involvement in this Iraq-Iran war and what some might consider an Iranian Holocaust [14] Mamoud Ahmadinejad denies the

---

[14] Some might prefer an analogy with the First World War. I do not use the term lightly. The war included ethnic cleansing and WMD and mass murder.

Oxford Dictionary: *holocaust noun*

> *1 destruction or slaughter on a mass scale, esp. caused by fire or nuclear war: a nuclear holocaust | the threat of imminent holocaust.*

> *(the Holocaust) the mass murder of Jews under the German*

Nazi regime during the period 1941–45. More than 6 million European Jews, as well as members of other persecuted groups, such as gypsies and homosexuals, were murdered at concentration camps such as Auschwitz.

2 historical a Jewish sacrificial offering that is burned completely on an altar.

ORIGIN Middle English: from Old French holocauste, via late Latin from Greek holokauston, from holos 'whole' + kaustos 'burned' (from kaiein 'burn').

Holocaust Thesaurus:

noun

fears of a nuclear holocaust cataclysm, disaster, catastrophe; destruction, devastation, annihilation; massacre, slaughter, mass murder, extermination, extirpation, carnage, butchery; genocide, ethnic cleansing, pogrom.

It was genocide according to Article 2 of the UN convention on genocide states:

In the present Convention, genocide means any of the following acts committed with intent to destroy, in whole or in part, a national, ethnical, racial or religious group, as such:

(a) Killing members of the group;

(b) Causing serious bodily or mental harm to members of the group;(c) Deliberately inflicting on the group conditions of life calculated to bring about its physical destruction in whole or in part; (d) Imposing measures intended to prevent births within the group;(e) Forcibly transferring children of the group to another group.

occurrence of the Jewish Holocaust.[15] It is fruitless to object that Iran did not suffer on the same scale. Holocausts are not defined by size. The twin towers victims died a horrible death in a holocaust as did hundreds of thousands soldiers who died in the Iraq-Iran war. (See Graham Greene 1955 *The Quiet American* Heinemann Ltd and in association with Penguin books 1977 *'Suffering is not increased by numbers: one body can contain all the suffering the world can feel.'* p. 183).

Mahmoud Ahmadinejad joins the ranks of holocaust/genocide deniers, who are often selective in their recognition of holocausts. Although the primary responsibility for the war rests with Iraq one might consider the context and provocation provided by U.S. support for Iraq and the relative silence about Iran's suffering as a means of understanding why such attitudes might occur.

---

[15] There are dissident views in Iran, see Wikipedia on Iranian conference http://en.wikipedia.org/wiki/International_Conference_to_Review_the_Glo bal_Vision_of_the_Holocaust. It is worth noting that the Ayatollah Khomeini issued a religious edict against such weapons see *http://www.uruknet.info/?p=m23254&l=i&size=1&hd=0* 'The Nuclear Non- Proliferation Treaty Is Dead' *K Gajendra Singh December 22 2006*. For other views on Iran's complicity in 'terror' there is a more U.S. viewpoint at: http://www.globalsecurity.org/wmd/library/news/iran/2006/26-180706.htm

On an advanced planet even heads of state would be brought to trial for holocaust or genocide denial and/or cover up.

In no way do I support this denial of the Jewish Holocaust. Indeed it is extremely reprehensible.[16] Mahmoud Ahmadinejad might have drawn other conclusions considering the military aid received from Israel. But the shock Iran received from the war drove it into nativistic[17] fundamentalism, in much the same way that Cambodia was shocked into Pol Pot's nativism by similar acts of war instigated by Kissinger and Nixon. (I do not think that a socio-psychological background (pace Hollywood) is an excuse. Hussein's psychopathology can only be understood in

---

[16] It might best be dealt with by inviting him to Auschwitz and Belsen rather than shouting at him over CNN.

[17] Ralph Linton 1943 Nativistic movements *American Anthropologist* **45** No. 2: 230-240

answers.com:

> *nativism, in anthropology, social movement that proclaims the return to power of the natives of a colonized area and the resurgence of native culture, along with the decline of the colonizers...One of the earliest careful studies of nativism was that of James Mooney (1896), who studied the Ghost Dance among Native Americans...*

Usually only considered in relation to small-scale pre-industrial societies, however it is extremely useful in understanding mass nationalistic fundamentalist responses in 20th and 21st centuries.

the context of his personal history, but this does not diminish his responsibility for war crimes).[18]

It is worth stating that during their support for Iraq the U.S. military shot down an Iranian civilian airline with a loss of all 290 passengers. The U.S. paid compensation but offered no apology. Imagine the U.S. response if Iran did the same. Iran would most likely have been bombed. [19]

For an account of the despicable behaviour of many nations in the conflict see☐ 'The United States and The Iran-Iraq War' Stephen R. Shalom 1990: *http://www.zmag.org/zmag/articles/ShalomIranIraq.htm*.

---

[18] See Thomas Keneally's parsimony in psychological explanations about Hitler *Gossip from the Forest* 1985 Harvest Books. Nixon and Kissinger, in their illegal bombing of Cambodia and the mass murder of over a million citizens, caused a convulsive Nativistic response and the emergence of Pol Pot. See *Sideshow: Kissinger, Nixon and the Destruction of Cambodia* William Shawcross, Simon and Schuster, 1979. This understanding does not condone Pol Pot's actions.

[19] This indicates that superior weaponry is actually dictating policy more than rationality. The Bush administration should stop thinking with its weapons.

CHAPTER FOUR THE FIRST GULF WAR

In the first gulf war 1991 in which the U.S. led a large coalition against Iraq to 'liberate' Kuwait, it is said that 85,000 people died. This does not include subsequent deaths.

Following the war the sanctions applied to Iraq from 1990 killed 500,000 children:

> *In strict contravention of the Geneva Convention, all 'necessary to sustain life' was destroyed within the first hours of bombing (January 17th 1991) water, electricity, health infrastructure, communications, schools, food stores, large scale farms, productions units, bridges, roads, all industrial infrastructure. All needed for repair was denied under the U.S. /UK driven embargo. During 1991, 'baseline mortality for the under fives, rose from 43.2 per thousand to 128.5 per thousand. A formerly largely well-nourished nation was being compared in health and diet, to Mali and other of the world's poorest countries, according to the UN Food and Agriculture Organization. An estimated one and a half million souls died from 'embargo related causes', to the 2003 invasion.*

> *On 1st January 1996, Ramsey Clark, twice U.S. Attorney General, wrote to all Members of the UN Security Council: 'There is one crime against humanity in this last decade of the millennium, that exceeds all others in magnitude, cruelty and*

portent. It is the US-forced sanctions against the twenty million people of Iraq.' A detailed, shaming depiction of Iraqis plight, concludes: ' You must vote against these genocidal sanctions. Your nations should not share responsibility for the deaths of more than ten thousand Iraqis who will die before the Security Council Review in March, if sanctions are not lifted in January.' The shameful world body, avowed to protect 'succeeding generations', voted to maintain sanctions. The previous year, the head of the Red Cross told Clark that in one week, there had been six thousand infant deaths from diaharrea and vomiting due to contaminated water. Rehydration and antibiotics costing just cents a dose, would have saved most. They were blocked under US-UK pressure. 'The enjoyment of the highest standard of health is… the fundamental right of every human being...' states the constitution of the (UN) World Health Organization. (November 26, 2006 Crimes against Humanity in the Middle East Who are the War Criminals? Felicity Arbuthnot Global Research, November 10, 2006: http://www.globalresearch.ca/index.php?context=viewArticle&code=ARB20061110&articleId=3790*).*

It serves little purpose to defeat evil with a greater evil. Hussein remained unmoved by the plight of his people and benefited from the sanctions.

CHAPTER FIVE THE SECOND GULF WAR

Begun in 2003 the present war used WMD and terrorism as a pretext for invasion. The world cannot be safe when there are double standards in international affairs and the NPT is not honoured e.g. if we don't want WMD then we must get rid of ours.

OUR WMD

A BBC article refers to the Bush Blair commitment to WMD into the 2040s. 'The White Paper on the Future of Trident proposes to spend 20 billion pounds.'

(at http://news.bbc.co.uk/1/hi/uk_politics/6197711.stm).

Blair's statement to parliament in full can be found here: http://news.bbc.co.uk/1/hi/uk_politics/6207584.stm.

Britain has four Vanguard submarines, each with sixteen Trident missiles. That is 64 WMD, each equivalent to eight Hiroshimas i.e. a total of 512 Hiroshimas. Estimates of the deaths at Hiroshima vary between 92,000 and 200,000. If we assume a figure of 100,000, that is enough warheads to murder 51 million people immediately, without deaths from f   a   l   l   o   u   t (http://en.wikipedia.org/wiki/Atomic_bombings_of_Hiroshima_and_Nagas a   k   i   )   .

Britain has another 70 missiles in store. Each submarine can carry 12 missiles, very useful for taking out a terrorist in Croydon. Missile details from the BBC website:

Length: 44ft (13m)

Weight: 130,000lb (58,500kg)

Diameter: 74 inches (1.9m)

Range: More than 4,600 miles (7,400km)

Power plant: Three stage solid propellant rocket

Cost: £16.8m ($29.1m) per missile

Source: Federation of American Scientists

Full facts at: http://news.bbc.co.uk/1/hi/uk/4438392.stm. This page contains a very useful search engine for other military facts including 'Bunker Busting' bombs).

In a further article on Nuclear disarmament (http://news.bbc.co.uk/1/hi/world/6103398.stm) the BBC quotes the following damming facts on the possession of nuclear weapons:

United States:

70,000 produced since 1945

10,000 in current stockpile (5,735 operational)

Russia:

55,000 produced since 1949

16,000 in current stockpile (5,830 operational)

Britain:

1,200 produced since 1953

Fewer than 200 Trident missiles remain

France

1,260 produced since 1964

350 in current stockpile

China

600 produced since 1964

Approx 200 in current stockpile (approx 130 deployed)

Source: All figs are estimates from Bulletin of Atomic Scientists (July 2006)

This article also quotes Article VI of the NPT:

Each of the Parties to the Treaty undertakes to pursue negotiations in good faith on effective measures relating to cessation of the nuclear arms race at an early date and to nuclear disarmament, and on a Treaty on general and

29

complete disarmament under strict and effective
international control.

Yet the signatories to the Treaty are actively developing their nuclear weapons, as are non-signatory states like Pakistan and India.

It would appear that there is a terrifying double standard governing whose nuclear weapons are approved and whose are not. Falk (Milbank Professor of International Law Emeritus, Princeton University) writes:

> *In my view, the greatest mind-game of our era is the degree to which the nuclear weapons states have convinced most of the world that the danger of these weapons arises from the countries that don't possess them rather than from the countries that do.[20] It is an incredible intellectual and political feat to have shifted the burden away from those countries that have developed and possess these weapons, in one case have actually used them, and continue to insist that they have the right to retain them, and even refuse to take off the table their possible future use. It's an extraordinary mind-game that most of us, including most of the people in the peace movement, have quietly accepted and have settled for, saying, "well, let's slow down*

---

[20] See William Blum 2000 *Rogue State; A Guide to the World's Only Super Power* Common Courage Press see reviews at
http://www.amazon.com/Rogue-State-Guide-Worlds-Superpower/dp/1567511945

the nuclear arms race" or "let's stabilize at a lower level existing arsenals of nuclear weapons, but let's devote ourselves mainly to the perils of nuclear proliferation." I think that this is a dangerous course to take, as well as being a politically futile and morally sterile approach to what should be our main preoccupations—that is, preventing the threat or use of these weapons by anyone ever and of creating a safer and fairer world...

In the present setting this American crime of aggressive war has been waged to keep other countries from acquiring the weapons that we continue to possess and develop. Further, the Non-Proliferation Treaty (NPT), to the extent that it represents the embodiment of international law in this area, has been materially breached by the nuclear weapon states, and any country that wishes, could without even relying on the withdrawal provision in Article X of the Treaty, regard the whole agreement as void. The nuclear weapons states are obliged in Article VI to commit themselves to seek nuclear disarmament in good faith and then to go further, and attempt to negotiate general and complete disarmament. This commitment is undertaken by the nuclear weapons states in exchange for the agreement of non-nuclear weapons states to forego their own weapons option. This Article VI commitment was treated as a fundamental premise of the NPT, being affirmed unanimously by the International Court of Justice in its seminal Advisory Opinion of 1996, a view supported fully even by the US judge on the court. The refusal of the nuclear weapons states to implement this commitment casts a long *shadow over any insistence that the non-nuclear states continue to be bound by the treaty.*

The second difficulty is the extremely discriminatory manners in which this treaty has been interpreted and applied over the years. Germany and Japan developed a complete nuclear fuel cycle without encountering the slightest opposition, while Iran is being threatened with war because Iran is seeking to possess the kind of peaceful nuclear energy technology that it is promised by Article IV of the NPT (At the Nuclear Precipice: Nuclear Weapons and the Abandonment of International Law International Law Symposium – Public Forum Thursday, February 23, 2006 Speaker: Dr. Richard Falk http://www.wagingpeace.org/articles/2006/02/23 falk nuclear-precipice.htm

In my view it is preposterous that most nuclear-armed states have convinced so many that their weapons are not a threat and that countries without them are, including one state that has in place a religious prohibition forbidding their use.

A single standard should apply to all and universal nuclear disarmament pursued as a matter of urgency, as demanded by the NPT and by the altered facts of the world. No purpose is served by their possession. On the contrary their possession is an inducement to other states to develop such weapons in self-defense and, thereby, create the insecurity they are meant to prevent.

All nuclear weapons should be considered to be immoral and unthinkable.

MORAL POSTURING

The past history of U.S., U.K., Australian active and tacit, support for Hussein's WMD and biological weapons utterly refutes any current moral posturing.

These countries and others supported Hussein in the past and in the current occupation of Iraq, have committed crimes, which they denounce when committed by other nations. The same countries, which supported Hussein for many years now parade themselves as virtuous defenders of freedom and democracy.

Australia fought in the Vietnam War and at best was pretty quiet about the war against Iran and now is actively engaged in the current occupation of Iraq. The Australian Prime Minister John Howard, unrepentant about Vietnam, is also apparently afflicted by the same lack of policy and information as Bush and is also implicated in crimes against humanity. He has a record of prevarication. And in a peculiar anachronism he remains a supporter of the Vietnam War (see Adams, P.: 'Our reckless deranged leader' *The Australian* 28 November 2006). There are many parallels between Vietnam and the current war in Iraq.[21]

---

[21] The analogy with Vietnam is a good one. There was no clear divide in Vietnam at all. 'Communist' insurgents and other factions were everywhere and there were many competing factions in the south. President Johnson tragically escalated the war in the mistaken belief that more bombs and troops would win the war.

This was an illegal war in which many innocent people perished and during which America committed many war crimes including ecocide. Hersh, Seymour M., in 1997 in *The Dark Side of Camelot.* shows how Kennedy was dominated by his reactionary father and prevented the cessation of the Vietnam war at its earlier stages. This is essential reading for anyone who wishes to be well informed about these matters. It did not progress the collapse of communism one iota and cost U.S. and the world dearly. The U.S. has never apologized nor its wrongs. Nor has any recognized International War Crimes tribunal sat in judgement. The great British philosopher Bertrand Russell inaugurated the Russell Tribunal in 1966, 1967 in Stockholm see Wikipedia; http://en.wikipedia.org/wiki/Russell Tribunal see also Vietnam War casualties with Google search and http://en.wikipedia.org/wiki/Vietnam War

Bush, under guidance from Kissinger and God (an unlikely pair), is making the same fatal error and escalating the war.

See also Bao Ninh 1995 *The Sorrow of War* Minerva, a novel from the North Vietnam point of view translated by Frank Palmer. The Independent said that this ranked alongside the greatest war novel of the 20th Century Erich Maria Remarques 1929 *All Quiet on the Western Front.*

War is reproduced in many spousal conflicts and seared into the lives of children for many generations in many ways. I was

34

In his support for U.S. policy he helped create the immigration crisis, which he capitalized, through the Tampa deception[22], into an election success.

In another apparent example of plausible deniability he apparently failed to notice that when his government was attacking Hussein Australia was also selling him huge quantities of wheat. One did not need an enquiry to point out that this contradiction should have been obvious to the tiniest intellect at the time.

It is proof of a craven, indolent, decadent media and then comatose opposition that it was not pursued at the time.

Howard remains a supporter of the Iraq occupation despite the indisputable refutation of the excuse for the war- the WMD. The goals of the war- to eliminate WMD, to free Iraq and to make Americans safer from terrorism, were based on entirely fanciful rhetorical paradigms of the region and, post hoc, were rationalized into a domino theory of democracy.

---

born in 1939 and did not stop drawing dogfights for seven years after the war and have spent my life in fear of it, opposing wars and trying to find a safe haven.

[22] 'Illegal' boat migrants were falsely accused of throwing their children overboard to save themselves. Howard's defence was that his underlings did not tell him of the true circumstances.

Bush seems to have fallen into a trap. Bin Laden is a superior chess player and Bush reacted predictably to 9/11, so Bin Laden turned him onto a recruiting agent. Thus the Bush's remained friends of the family.[23]

IDEOLOGICAL JUSTIFICATION

All great violence in the 20th century was preceded by ideological justification. The justification of the present occupation was also ideological. After the attack on the Twin Towers someone had to pay, so began the cut and pastiche war with phrases readily traced to cold war rhetoric, the terms: *'The War on Terror'*, *'The Axis of Evil'* [24] were plagiarized from Reagan's *'Empire of Evil'* and other sources. A collaged ideology was thereby harnessed to fathomless stupidity.

The *New York Review of Books* calls it the 'War of the Imagination'. It is rather a war of delirium-resembling a bricolage of faintly remembered shards of the disasters of 20th century history extracted from the febrile hallucinations of a dying man.

---

[23] Search Google: Bush Family and Bin Ladens.

[24] For those who need a challenging perspective on this nonsense find what Omid Djalili the comedian has to say check out his web site and the BBC on Iran http://www.bbc.co.uk/radio4/iran/

GOD ON OUR SIDE

Blair and Bush have also grafted the rhetoric of the cold war into an imaginary battle of good against evil, pitting their God [25] against the God of the fundamentalists. This is a ludicrous dichotomy, which reflects their religious hubris and delusions of grandeur.[26] The rhetoric of good and evil serves no purpose.[27]

---

[25] Goldberg writes in his critical review of Carter's new book: *Palestine: Peace Not Apartheid* Simon & Schuster 2006:

> *Carter succeeded at his Camp David summit in 1978, while Clinton failed at his in 2000. But Clinton's achievement was in some ways greater because he did something no American president has done before (or since): He won the trust of both the Palestinians and the Israelis. He could do this because he seemed to believe that neither side was wholly villainous nor wholly innocent. He saw the Israeli-Palestinian crisis for what it is: a tragic collision between right and right, a story of two peoples who both deserved his sympathy. In other words, he took the Christian approach to making peace.*

[26] They have both fallen into the trap of believing that the office they occupy confers wisdom. This is hubris at its worst.

[27] Machin, B. discusses the phenomenon of projection in 1986 *The Moral Premises of Nuclear War.* In Maas, J. P., and Steward, R. A. (Eds.). *Toward A World of Peace: People Create Alternatives.* Proceedings of the First International Conference on Conflict Resolution and Peace Studies. University of the South Pacific, Suva, Fiji. The abstract reads:

We are often trapped in the preconceptions of a system of thought. The arms race is a moral issue with historical, social and psychological roots. This paper examines the thinking behind it: the myth of scientific expertise; the myth of the external present; the conceptual status of' the 'other'; the consequences of defensiveness and its acceptable levels; the premise of mass genocide; the rights of children; the damage inflicted by undropped bombs; the harm inflicted by dual codes, and legitimate and illegitimate 'terrorism' The more the projections of evil continue the worse the situation will become.

In this article Machin writes:

Non-Christian natives were by definition allied to the demonic, evil and inhuman category of beings. Bodley (1975) estimates 50 million tribal people perished between 1780 and 1930. The murder of Latin American Indians began much earlier of course; the foundation of this exploration and extermination was a categorization of Otherness.

Otherness and projection of evil, the Satanizing of the victim seem inevitable components of state formation.

In the twentieth century these crusading murderous tendencies have reached new heights of perfection culminating in the holocaust of the Second World War (Kenrick and Puxon, 1972). Hiroshima and Nagasaki were only possible by a similar kind of exclusion - as a race beyond the pale with antihuman characteristics. The Japanese, as much as anything else, were punished for having different definitions of conduct and contrasting concepts of the person.

The demonizing of the 'Other' is a necessary component of the most bestial human behaviour, stripping away the last vestiges of civilized behaviour, appealing to the basest

Bush apparently takes his guidance from God at morning prayer. He might bear in mind Matthew 5:43:

> *Ye have heard that it hath been said, Thou shalt love thy neighbour, and hate thine enemy. But I say unto you, Love your enemies, bless them that curse you, do good to them that hate you, and pray for them which despitefully use you, and persecute you;*

He might also consider the circumstances in which this advice was given, and Leviticus 19:18:

> *You shall not take vengeance or bear a grudge against any of your people, but you shall love your neighbor as yourself: I am the Lord.*

The tragedy is all combatants believe that God is on their side and will ensure victory. How can this be if there is only one God? If there is only one God then he must have created the many different cultures and nations and belief systems. Each population and religion must therefore be a refraction of a single numinous God. A creator of the infinite universe

---

> *bigotry and ignorance and tearing away the rules and conveniences of war that have so frequently governed face to face conflict between men, creating groups of people to whom the rules of conduct including the rules of war cease to apply ... Because of their imagined crimes they cease to be seen as human beings and as a consequence may be submitted even in the imagination to the most mind-defying inhuman acts.*

This is available as a mobipocket ebook and on lulu.com.

would probably view the difference between nations as parents would view squabbles between siblings.

CESSATION OF MORALITY

Why is it that in war moral judgments cease and what is indefensible and criminal in one's own country becomes the measure of heroism and national honour in the territory of another? Why does morality cease to exist beyond one's own borders?

Why is it that Nationalism precludes rational thought? Why is such immorality dressed up as if it were noble and pure and coming from God when in fact it stems from the basest motives of greed and vengeance?

The support of this war is cynical, repulsive, ignoble and godless, continued by empty justification, lies and, on some sides, the pleasure of murder.[28]

CASUALTIES

---

[28] The Sunday Times January 21, 2007 'Is this Iraq's most prolific mass killer' Jon Swain, Baghdad. This is about *'Abu Deraa, an elusive Shi'ite whose orgy of sectarian killings in the past two years has helped to propel Iraq towards civil war'*. There are such men who have used the war as an excuse to satisfy their bloodlust and religious hatred.

In this tardy Iraq war of liberation led by U.S.A., U.K. and Australia the initial casualties were supposedly 14,000.

For the current casualties see http://www.antiwar.com/casualties/. The U.S. casualties are between 23,000-100,000 (http://www.antiwar.com/casualties/list.php). The Lancet estimates 100,000 Iraqi civilian casualties. Other estimates put them as high as 655,000☐

> *From wars on babies to wars on the devastated: the inevitable, illegal invasion of Iraq. John Hopkins School of Public Health's meticulous Professor Les Roberts, estimates a possible further six hundred and fifty five thousand excess deaths in Iraq - or more - due to rape, torture, destruction on a barely believable scale; hospitals which now seem well stocked under the embargo's horrors, 'Falluja's' across ancient Mesopotamia in the name of the U.S. and UK, for which no one is held responsible, killing Iraqis: '... choosing to die resisting... (fleeing) only from dishonor.' Or just for being Iraqi (Arbuthnot op. cit.).*

In *The New York Review of Books* 2006 Volume 53, Number 20 • December 21, 2006 Iraq: 'The War of the Imagination' Mark Danner reviews three books: *State of Denial: Bush at War*, Part III Bob Woodward, *The One Percent Doctrine: Deep Inside America's Pursuit of Its Enemies Since 9/11* Ron Suskind, *State* of War: The Secret History of the CIA and the Bush Administration James Risen.[29] He writes:

> As Iraqis know well, the power drills and nails were a favorite of Saddam's torturers—though now, according to a United Nations expert on torture, "the situation is so bad many people say it is worse than it has been in the times of Saddam Hussein."[12] The level of carnage is difficult to comprehend. According to official figures published by the United Nations, which certainly understate the case, 6,599 Iraqis were murdered in July and August alone. Estimates of the number of Iraqi civilians killed during the war range from a conservative 52,000, by the Web site Iraq Body Count, to 655,000 by the Johns Hopkins School of Public Health, with the Iraqi Health Minister recently announcing a cumulative total of 150,000. [13] Worst of all the US has created the current civil war and insurgency.

As Danner says Bush was impatient with considered policy analysis and complex information and reacted as if they were an impediment to decisive action.

---

[29] Also very relevant is 'Defiant Iran' Christopher de Bellaigue reviewing: *Confronting Iran: The Failure of American Foreign Policy and the Next Great Crisis in the Middle East* Ali M. Ansari Basic Books, *Hidden Iran: Paradox and Power in the Islamic Republic* Ray Takeyh *New York Review of Books* Volume 53, Number 17 · November 2, 2006.

As I recall his wife said that, 'George's answer to everything is to take out the chainsaw'.

The current civil war was made inevitable by the deliberate dismantling of the organs of social order through the disastrous de-Baathification and demilitarization.

Danner says Bremer gave the order to remove all Baathist members:

> *Garner, who will shortly be going home, sees he's making little headway and appeals to the CIA man, who "had been station chief in other Middle East countries," asking him what will happen if the order is issued.*
>
> *"If you put this out, you're going to drive between 30,000 and 50,000 Baathists underground before nightfall," Charlie said.... "You will put 50,000 people on the street, underground and mad at Americans." And these 50,000 were the most powerful, well-connected elites from all walks of life.*
>
> *"I told you," Bremer said, looking at Charlie. "I have my instructions and I have to implement this...*
>
> *The following day, Bremer's second in Iraq, the hapless Garner was handed another draft order. This, Woodward tells us, was Order Number 2, disbanding the Iraqi ministries of Defense and Interior, the entire Iraqi military, and all of Saddam's bodyguard and special paramilitary organization.*

Garner was stunned. The de-Baathification order was dumb, but this was a disaster. Garner had told the president and the whole National Security Council explicitly that they planned to use the Iraqi military—at least 200,000 to 300,000 troops—as the backbone of the corps to rebuild the country and provide security. And he'd been giving regular secure video reports to Rumsfeld and Washington on the plan.

…"Jerry," it might be said at this point, seems a well-meaning man, but he had never run anything larger than the United States embassy in the Netherlands, where he served as ambassador. He spoke no Arabic and knew little of the Middle East and nothing of Iraq. He had had nothing to do with the meager and inadequate planning the Pentagon had done for "the postwar" and indeed had had only a few days' preparation before being flown to Baghdad. He apparently never saw the extensive plans the State Department had drawn up for the postwar period. And as would become evident as the occupation wore on and he became more independent of the Pentagon civilians, he had no particular qualifications to make and implement decisions of such magnitude, decisions that would certainly prolong the American occupation and would ultimately do much to doom it. For Rumsfeld, however, Bremer's supposed independence in Baghdad has had its uses.

Danner (ibid.) continues:

Nearly four years into the Iraq war, as we enter the Time of Proposed Solutions, the consequences of those early decisions define the bloody landscape. By dismissing and humiliating the soldiers and officers of the Iraqi army our leaders, in effect, did much to recruit the insurgency. By bringing far too few troops to secure Saddam's enormous arms depots they armed it. By bringing too few to keep order they presided over the looting and overwhelming violence and social disintegration that provided the insurgency such fertile soil. By blithely purging tens of thousands of the country's Baathist elite, whatever their deeds, and by establishing a muscle-bound and inept American occupation without an "Iraqi face," they created an increasing resentment among Iraqis that fostered the insurgency and encouraged people to shelter it. And by providing too few troops to secure Iraq's borders they helped supply its forces with an unending number of Sunni Islamic extremists from neighboring states. It was the foreign Islamists' strategy above all to promote their jihadist cause by provoking a sectarian civil war in Iraq; by failing to prevent their attacks and to protect the Shia who became their targets, the US leaders have allowed them to succeed.

With two chains of command, little communication between the State department and the Pentagon, a secretive and bungling Secretary of Defence and a President, who apparently does not wish to be impeded by information or significant discussion of policy, the U.S. proceeded down the road to hell, creating the very conditions for fundamentalist takeover of the Middle East it wished to avoid.

Danner's article shows that factual information from Iraq was virtually non-existent and what little there was was filtered and interpreted whimsically by in the Pentagon. Very little intelligence was reaching the Oval Office and none was coming out of it.

At the centre of the apparent desire to create a 'tsunami of democracy' was the paradox of an unelected inexperienced fool creating nonsensical policy, which provided the mass basis for insurgency, which might not otherwise have existed.

Behind this dreadful fiasco was Rumsfeld, who rarely spoke with Rice and used an intermediary to carry out his machinations his decisions, presumably so he could plausibly deny he was responsible.

What is readily apparent from all accounts is the failure of the U.S. administration to grasp the complexities and realities of Iraqi culture.

As the review by Christian Caryl 'What About the Iraqis?' shows in the *New York Review of Books* Volume 54, Number 1 • January 11, 2007, *Baghdad Burning: Girl Blog from Iraq* Riverbend, with a foreword by Ahdaf Soueif and an introduction by James Ridgeway, *Baghdad Burning II: More Girl Blog from Iraq* Riverbend, with an introduction by James Ridgeway and Jean Cassella, *Night Draws Near: Iraq's People in the Shadow of America's War* Anthony Shadid, Picador, *In the Belly of the Green Bird: The Triumph of the Martyrs in Iraq* Nir Rosen, Free Press.

Americans, by now, can be forgiven for believing that we know something about the situation in

Iraq; we hear about it, after all, every day, in what seems like benumbing detail. And yet, in reality, what we know about the lives of individual Iraqis rarely goes beyond the fleeting opinion quote or the civilian casualty statistics. We have little impression of Iraqis as people trying to live lives that are larger and more complex than the war that engulfs them, and more often than not we end up viewing them merely as appendages of conflict. The language of foreign policy abstraction and a misplaced sense of decorum on the part of the press and television also conspire to sanitize the fantastically disgusting realities of everyday death. One of Riverbend's neighbors has been missing ever since he drove off one day in April as American troops were entering the city. His family has spent the past five months trying to determine his final fate.

The Iraqi government itself includes the Islamist Dawa Party responsible for car bombings in the 1980s.

As Shadid recounts the occupation is felt to be repugnant even when Iraqis were pleased about Saddam's removal.

There has been little serious attempt to gauge Iraqi public opinion and its complex culture and current divisions (see also Thomas Ricks *Fiasco: The American Military Adventure in Iraq* Penguin, 2006).

The administration has systematically ignored opinions and knowledge, which contradicted its hardened views.

The FBI and CIA are inadequately staffed with people fluent in the language and culture.

The U.S. seriously underestimates the Mahdi army and the influence of Moqtada al-Sadr whose help, in my opinion, must be enlisted to achieve any kind of order in Iraq.

In January the discussion about an increase in U.S. troops constantly refers to the possibility of civil war if foreign troops are withdrawn. The Iraqis know that there is no doubt that the civil war has already started, as this review states:

> As I listened to these Iraqi voices, I could not entirely shake the feeling that we Americans are already becoming irrelevant to the future of their country. While people in Washington continue to debate the next change in course, and the Baker report raises the possibility of gradual withdrawal, Iraqis are sizing up the coming apocalypse, and making their arrangements accordingly. My conversations with those hapless Baghdadis took place under a glowering afternoon sky that announced the arrival of the rainy season. It was the day that an Iraqi tribunal pronounced a verdict of death for Saddam Hussein, news marked by a crackle of celebratory gunfire somewhere in the distance. Aside from that, though, no one really seemed to care; they are worried about saving their own lives.

CHAPTER SIX EVERY DAY IS 9/11

The U.S. was rightly horrified by 9/11 but this does not justify the commission of, or complicity in, similar or worse crimes on other populations.

Every day is 9/11 in Iraq and the intervention of the 'coalition of the willing' has compounded the damage to innocent civilians. From the support of the Iraq-Iran war onwards many participating countries can be held responsible for up to a million dead, including over 500,000 children.

The deliberate use of Uranium-depleted bombs ranks amongst the worst of crimes. The Augustus Richard Norton review of *The Great War for Civilisation* by Robert Fisk book *The Nation* magazine, February 6, 2006 states:

> In the area around Basra in southern Iraq, to take one of many examples in Fisk's book, there has been a phenomenal epidemic of leukemia, breast and stomach cancer presumably connected to the introduction of an estimated 340 tons of radioactive material into the environment during the 1991 Gulf War. The source of the radioactivity? The profligate use of depleted uranium ammunition by the US military. In areas where the ammunition was fired in great quantities, cancer rates in children are as high as 71.8 per 100,000 compared with a regional average of 3.9 per 100,000. An Iraqi doctor reviewing his patient files tells Fisk, "Of fifteen

cancer patients from one area, I have only two left. I am receiving children with cancer of the bone--this is incredible... My God, I have performed mastectomies on two girls with cancer of the breast--one of them was only fourteen years old." Fisk calls this the product of "a policy of bomb now, die later."

Every child that dies is our child. Every child's death is an intolerable murder. One such collateral death is one too many. What possible comfort can this be to the dead of 9/11? - *'You killed my children, so I burned your children accidentally because Al Qaeda bombed the Twin Towers?'* This is vendetta gone mad. Every death adds to the hatred, which the insurgents must feel for the occupiers. Hatred we would share if they were our children. And they are all our children.

There is no use is excusing such deaths by saying they were unintentional, nor by saying that the deaths were an unfortunate necessity or the consequence of a noble purpose. There can be nothing righteous or justifiable about a child's death.

Add the latest civilian casualties to the deaths in the Iraq-Iran war, the Gulf wars and the sanctions and here is a sum for you: how many 9/11s does that make? How many children need to die to build a bridge for democracy? (Greene op.cit. on the Vietnam War: *A two-hundred-pound bomb does not discriminate. How many dead colonels justify a child's or a trishaw driver's death when you are building a national democratic front? p.162.* The home- guard hero should remember Vietnam was the war for democracy he avoided).[30]

---

[30] Hamas was democratically elected, and the United States refuses to deal with them. I thought they are conducting the Iraq war for democracy. I understand the Hamas position on Israel makes it difficult.

Among the reasons for Hamas success was founded in the corruption of the Arafat Palestinian Authority - a corruption tolerated by the U.S. despite the flagrant disregard of democratic institutions. You sew what you reap. Hamas offered a truce. In my belief peace and ten years of affluence will bring about Hamas recognition of Israel. Theirs is a patently untenable position. Israel justifiably will resist them with all their might. But this resistance must not include crimes against humanity. Illegal acts should include the use of cluster bombs and the doctrine of collective responsibility. For those who remember from Vietnam cluster bombs were designed to continue to travel within the body after impact.

Terror is indivisible. It is insupportable on both sides. All states should cease acts of violence against innocent men, women and children. All racial discrimination should be illegal. Hezbollah should stop its campaign of civilian bombings and its cynical location of its attacks in civilian districts. It should consider changing completely and adopting Ghandian tactics.

It is tragic to see the innocents killed on both sides and the escalating hatreds and mutual incomprehension. Israel will never allow another Holocaust and will resist all organizations, which refuse to accept its existence. Currently there is the dreadful rumour that Israel will employ bunker-busting nuclear weapons in Iran *The Sunday Times* January 07, 2007 'Revealed: Israel plans nuclear strike on Iran' Uzi Mahnaimi, New York and Sarah Baxter, Washington. This must be resisted. It is the moral equivalent of dropping Zyklon B.

(To refer to a later point -arms control is essential- Hezbollah, for example, is using latest Russian weaponry).

Hamas and Hezbollah and Iran must, of course, relinquish their irrational demand for the destruction of Israel. Organizations and states have to come to terms with the fact that some demands are utterly unrealistic and bound to produce an endless cycle of violence. Their hatred devours their own children.

If two people sat down to iron out differences and one said that the premise for discussion was the annihilation of the other there could be no hope for reconciliation or the end to suffering. This does make dialogue extremely difficult to say the least.

If Hamas and Hezbollah demands for the annihilation of Israel continue there can be no end to violence except mutual destruction and spiraling hatred as innocent blood is shed.

All wars and vendettas end even the most unspeakable horrors like the Holocaust, the fire bombing of Dresden and the dropping of the Atomic bombs on Japan have not prevented friendships between the bitterest of enemies. How much wiser to end this struggle sooner bypassing the thousands of shattered families and ruined lives on all sides, rather than endure relentless suffering and escalating reciprocal retaliation, hundreds of thousands of deaths and mutilations before crippled exhaustion brings an end. We are all brothers and sisters. This passage from *The Merchant of Venice* remains as relevant as ever:

SHYLOCK:

To bait fish withal. If it will feed nothing else, it will feed my revenge. He hath disgrac'd me and hind'red me half a million; laugh'd at my losses, mock'd at my gains, scorned my nation, thwarted my bargains, cooled my friends, heated mine enemies. And what's his reason? I am a Jew. Hath not a Jew eyes? Hath not a Jew hands, organs, dimensions,

Acts of war and the sanctions were intentional. Hundreds of thousands of children have died intentionally.

IMAGINE

Imagine that someone invades the U.S. on the pretext of finding WMD, after a similar act of violence; remember there are plenty of these to choose from not one. Note that in this scenario the excuse would not be a lie.

Imagine that the invasion destroys most of civil infrastructure: hospitals, schools, electricity, sewage and water.

---

senses, affections, passions, fed with the same food, hurt with the same weapons, subject to the same diseases, healed by the same means, warmed and cooled by the same winter and summer, as a Christian is? If you prick us, do we not bleed? If you tickle us, do we not laugh? If you poison us, do we not die? And if you wrong us, shall we not revenge? If we are like you in the rest, we will resemble you in that. If a Jew wrong a Christian, what is his humility? Revenge. If a Christian wrong a Jew, what should his sufferance be by Christian example? Why, revenge. The villainy you teach me I will execute; and it shall go hard but I will better the instruction.

For perhaps the most important and wisest example in modern times see Desmond Tutu 2000 *No Future Without Forgiveness: A Personal Overview of South Africa's Truth And Reconciliation Commission Rider* and Co.

The invaders promise to rebuild America and confiscate large amounts of U.S. money to do so, but the money is handed out to foreign contractors and the U.S. sees none of the reconstruction money.

Everyday the invaders kill large number of civilians in pursuit of the persons who perpetuated the original act. Persons who actually reside elsewhere.

Imagine endless killing of American children.

Imagine that insurgency quickly evolves and, given the invaders' superior weapons, heroic suicide bombings (resistance) follow.

The invaders adopt a policy of collectively responsibility and take vengeance on civilians, excusing the collateral damage, on high moral grounds, as a war against terror.

U.S. citizens who resist are branded terrorists. There are many different resistance groups, mirroring the complexity of American society.

This does not impress U.S. citizens who continue to press for the invaders to leave and continue stiff resistance.

Of course the U.S. insurgents do not regard the territory of the invaders as off reach. They do not want the citizens of the invading countries to believe they are safe. The U.S. is not safe, why should the invaders feel safe?

The invasion itself makes the war extend to the invaders' territory.

I suggest the U.K. and Australia try the same imaginary exercise.

CHAPTER SEVEN NEW PROPOSALS NEW DIRECTIONS

Explaining the context for terror does not excuse the terror but when the detail is revealed it is hard to portray the U.S. and U.K. as saviours or harbingers of decent civilization.

The sufferings of the Middle East were compounded by 9/11, which is fruitlessly branded into the sufferings of Iraq. Norton (op.cit.) reviewing Fisk again:

> But he insists on providing a context for Al Qaeda's atrocities, something that infuriates many people who prefer the convenient simplicity of a black-and-white world. He had the effrontery to suggest that U.S. policy, including its skewed stance on the Arab-Israeli conflict, has something to do with the enmity and distrust that America faces not just in the Middle East but in much of the world.

> No, Israel was not to blame for what happened on September 11th, 2001. The culprits were Arabs, not Israelis. But America's failure to act with honour in the Middle East, its promiscuous sale of missiles to those [i.e., the IDF in particular] who use them against civilians, its blithe disregard for the deaths of tens of thousands of Iraqi children under sanctions of which Washington was the principal supporter-- all these were intimately related to the society that produced the Arabs who plunged New York into an apocalypse of fire.

This is a war, based on lies and shifty morality, co-scripted by Douglas Adams, Joseph Heller, Al Capp and Dante.

It is a war, which must be halted immediately, and a major change of direction and thought substituted for the reflex chainsaw reaction.

In 'Better Late Than Never' Volume 54, Number 1 • January 11, *The New York Review of Books* review of James Baker *Work Hard, Study...and Keep Out of Politics! Adventures and Lessons from an Unexpected Public Life* and James A. Baker III, with Steve Fiffer Putnam. *The Iraq Study Group Report: The Way Forward—A New Approach* James A. Baker III and Lee H. Hamilton, co-chairs. Vintage, Michael Tomasky says:

> *It is not merely the recommendations, pushing the administration to lower troop levels, negotiate with Iran and Syria, and (most provocative of all) pressure Israel toward some accommodation with the Palestinians. The language of the report itself is clearly designed to say to the administration and the world: it's a failure. The first forty pages, called "Assessment," describe the realities on the ground in Iraq in merciless detail. The Iraqi army faces "significant questions" about the loyalty of units; the Iraqi police force is in "substantially worse" shape than the army. The political situation is close to hopeless; the economic situation is worse; U.S. reconstruction efforts have failed. The consequences of failure are described in terms more far-reaching than any I've seen: Ambassadors from neighboring countries told us that they fear the distinct*

possibility of Sunni-Shia clashes across the Islamic world. Many expressed a fear of Shia insurrections—perhaps fomented by Iran—in Sunni-ruled states. Such a broader sectarian conflict could open a Pandora's box of problems—including the radicalization of populations, mass movements of populations, and regime changes—that might take decades to play out...

Second, the report has set in motion the logic of withdrawal. ...

The real political problem in Iraq is one of national reconciliation—the Kurds want to be left alone, the Shiites want control after more than a thousand years, and as for the Sunnis, it's difficult to imagine them participating en masse in a federated republic. The ISG devotes fully fourteen of its recommendations to this important matter, chief among them a review of the Iraqi constitution, an accelerated de-Baathification process, and the development of a new oil revenue–sharing formula (for which a scheme was independently mooted by Iraqi leaders on December 8). The goals are the right ones, but they suggest a diplomatic process for which Iraqis have shown little enthusiasm, and the United States even less aptitude. Indeed it was a Sunni politician, Ayad al-Sammarai, who offered what might have been the sharpest, pithiest assessment of the report: "It is a report to solve American problems, and not to solve Iraq's problems."

I concur. All allied troops should withdraw. Instead of military engagement there should be a massive independently administered civilian 'Marshall Plan' and initially replacing the lost $23 billion.

Moqtada al-Sadr and all other significant Nationalist parties on the Sunni side have to be involved in the honest administration of this aid and participate in solutions. Al-Sadr is a nationalist and enjoyed some Sunni support

The first emphasis should be on providing and equipping large numbers of prefabricated and fully equipped field hospitals. [31] The current billion proposed by Bush is woefully inadequate compared to the an estimated $250 billion or more thus far spent on the war:

> *Patent economic failure is the price for the American failure to control the country. But that's not all. The cost of the war has exploded. The Bush administration had evaluated it at between 50 and 60 billion dollars in 2003. Meanwhile 251 billion dollars have already been spent according to a study by economists Laura Bilmes and (Nobel Prize winner) Joseph Stiglitz (le Prix Nobel), cited by the Financial Times' Martin Wolf. If the Bush administration decides to maintain the troops for another five years (even at a lower troop strength level), it will cost another 200 to 270 billion dollars. Adding the cost of care for the wounded, pensions, and replacement of military materiel, the bill rises to 750 billion or 1.2 trillion dollars: ten times the annual net development aid paid out by all rich countries.*

---

[31] These could immediately include large numbers of mobile truck-hospitals which are available in Japan and other countries.

> *For good measure, add in that the failure to produce Iraqi oil contributes to supply constraint and pushes prices up. The authors estimate the impact at $5 extra per barrel. Finally, they confess to renouncing any attempt to calculate other consequences, like the price of having enraged Muslims the world over or of the stain of Guantanamo on the United States' reputation. (The Other Failure in Iraq: The Economy Eric Le Boucher Le Monde Saturday 18 February 2006*

http://www.truthout.org/cgi-bin/artman/exec/view.cgi/47/17850).

I propose that the coalition concentrate on supporting the Iraqi government to embark on a program to consult and incorporate all key leaders of opposing groups and factions. The government of Iraq must include in its team of advisers real experts, not the sycophants like Chalabi the U.S. has hitherto preferred. It must consult Iraqi anthropologists, sociologists and historians and all the leaders of all factions. I suggest the Iraqi government can also listen to the people of Iraq directly (the proliferation of mobile phones should make that easy). The present Iraqi Prime Minister Nouri al-Maliki has suggested that Bush withdraw his troops to the outskirts of Baghdad and that his government be given sufficient weapons to carry out their peacekeeping tasks. This seems a sensible first step. In the Second World War the allies made the similar mistake of not arming the Cretans in their fight against the Germans and as a consequence the Germans occupied Crete.

A summit should be called for the regional powers, including Hamas and Hezbollah. The coalition should only advise but not participate at this summit.

America has no moral position on WMD. Bush should support the involvement of Iran in a cooperative and civil manner, apologizing for past misdeeds and promising a no-nuclear strike policy, at the same time requesting that the Mahmoud Ahmadinejad cease his intemperate language about Israel.

As Baker et al suggest Israel must be asked for concessions, but then so too must Hamas and Hezbollah, since a wider conflict will undoubtedly involve them.

Above all international law should be honoured and strengthened. Arms control, as Kofi Annan has suggested, must also play a central place in dampening the Middle East conflict.

This new Reasonpolitik is a substitute for the old Realpolitik.

Democracy cannot be spread on the basis of illusory Christian fundamentalism or on the mockery of democracy that the Bush administration policy and decision-making represents. Neither can it be spread or defended by a totally inappropriate recycling and rebranding of cold-war rhetoric, nor by delusions of moral superiority or nuclear double standards.

Unless universal standards of law and justice are applied the war is futile.[32] (Even U.S. constitutional standards applied on a global basis might be a good start).

Democracy can only be spread by universal, not culturally relative, international codes of law, justice and decency.[33]

---

[32] Clint Eastwood, in an interview about *Letters from Iwo Jima* 2006 recently said:

> *It's important to realize that war is a futile exercise at best, and people are trying to kill one another who, under other circumstances, could be extremely friendly. The Sunday Times December 10, 2006 How Clint recaptured the war movie.*

[33] http://www.globalpolicy.org/intljustice/icc/usindex.htm:

> *US Opposition to the International Criminal Court*
>
> *The United States government has consistently opposed an international court that could hold US military and political leaders to a uniform global standard of justice. The Clinton administration participated actively in negotiations towards the International Criminal Court treaty, seeking Security Council screening of cases. If adopted, this would have enabled the US to veto any dockets it opposed. When other countries refused to agree to such an unequal standard of justice, the US campaigned to weaken and undermine the court. The Bush administration, coming into office in 2001 as the Court neared implementation, adopted an extremely active opposition. Washington began to negotiate bilateral agreements with other countries, insuring immunity of US nationals from prosecution by the Court. As leverage, Washington threatened termination of economic aid,*

withdrawal of military assistance, and other painful measures. These exclusionary steps clearly endanger the fledgling Court and may seriously weaken its credibility and effectiveness.

The facts speak for themselves U.S. politicians' have committed major war crimes in Iraq as they did in Vietnam. (This is depressingly familiar. I spent much of my youth arguing against the Vietnam War).

I emphasize that all war crimes should be equal in International law and neither time nor nationality should bestow innocence. The U.S. crimes in Vietnam and Cambodia remain unpunished. Extant legislation backs my position. A universally applied law would place restraints on such violent policies and could mean that Rumsfeld could be tried for war crimes. Halliburton could be tried. Bush, Powell, Blair and Howard would not be immune from prosecution (Arbuthnot, F 2006 Who are the War Criminals ? http://www.globalresearch.ca/index.php?cotext=viewArticle&code=ARB20061110&articleId=3790). Even Kissinger might be asked to answer for his part in the bombing of Cambodia see Hitchens, C. 2002 *The trial of Henry Kissinger* Verso June and 2001 http://www.thirdworldtraveler.com/Kissinger/CaseAgainst1_Hitchens.html.

It seems incredible that Kissinger is currently influencing Bush. Behind all these war crimes, as in all crimes of murder, we have to ask what the motive is and this question leads to the arms manufacturers and others who profit from this and other wars. Cheyney, the vice-President, through his association with Halliburton, directly profited from the war.

There is a pressing need to vigorously pursue arms control i.e. both the 'legal' and illegal sale of arms. The arms dealers-the 'merchants of death' are the shadowy puppeteers. Think of the example of the grotesque amount of arms in the hands of the Iraqi population.

It might be suggested by some, although I couldn't possibly, that the G8 demonstrations are misplaced, and instead all arms manufacturers should be outed and hounded into their homes and children's schools and their lives made a misery until they cease their deathly merchandise. They should be treated by communities the same as pedophiles although their actions are far worse. They hand out the weapons and are therefore culpable accomplices to mass murder.

There is a famous trial in England when a young man was found guilty of murder through handing the weapon to the actual perpetrator:

> Derek Bentley was 19 when he was hanged for his part in the murder of Pc Sidney Miles in 1952 during a burglary that went wrong. Christopher Craig, his accomplice, fired the shot that killed Pc Miles after Bentley had been detained by another officer...

> But Craig, then 16, was too young to be hanged and at the Old Bailey trial officers testified that moments before the fatal shot Bentley had called out to his accomplice: "Let him have it, Chris." (UK News Electronic Telegraph Thursday 23 January 1997 Issue 608).

See also
http://www.boston.com/news/world/articles/2006/11/13/us_is_top_purveyo r_on_weapons_sales_list/ 'U.S. is the top purveyor on weapons sales list. Shipments grow to unstable areas' Bryan Bender, Globe Staff November 13, 2006 Boston Globe. The facts demonstrate that many nations are directly contributing to the instability they supposedly abhor.

Also   http://www.motherjones.com/news/special_reports/arms/   and:
http://www.nytimes.com/2006/10/29/world/europe/29weapons.html?ex=13 19774400&en=83c3ab9975b8b6d8&ei=5090

http://www.envirosagainstwar.org/know/read.php?itemid=4873

http://www.worldwatch.org/node/71

http://www.globalissues.org/Geopolitics/WarOnTerror/Disorder.asp.

Illegal arm's brokers:
http://www.iansa.org/issues/arms_brokers.htm

It would also mean Universal values and a true International Court. Such values and definitions would be applied to women and children. There could be a universal ban on honour crimes for example.

INDEX

www.ingramcontent.com/pod-product-compliance
Lightning Source LLC
Chambersburg PA
CBHW050601280326
41933CB00011B/1935